A Handful of Prayers

A Handful of Prayers

Poems and Sonnets for the End of Modernity

PETER LILLY

RESOURCE *Publications* · Eugene, Oregon

A HANDFUL OF PRAYERS
Poems and Sonnets for the End of Modernity

Copyright © 2024 Peter Lilly. All rights reserved. Except for brief quotations in critical publications or reviews, no part of this book may be reproduced in any manner without prior written permission from the publisher. Write: Permissions, Wipf and Stock Publishers, 199 W. 8th Ave., Suite 3, Eugene, OR 97401.

Resource Publications
An Imprint of Wipf and Stock Publishers
199 W. 8th Ave., Suite 3
Eugene, OR 97401

www.wipfandstock.com

PAPERBACK ISBN: 979-8-3852-0437-3
HARDCOVER ISBN: 979-8-3852-0438-0
EBOOK ISBN: 979-8-3852-0439-7

VERSION NUMBER 091924

'What came to nothing could always be replenished.
"Read poems as prayers," he said…'

Seamus Heaney

Contents

Dedication and Thanks | xi
Acknowledgements | xiii

Overture: Home as Place | 1

Legacy | 2
At Sea | 3
A-Perfect | 5
Spring | 6
Autumn Home | 7
Imagine the Water | 8
You Are His Place | 9

Poems and Sonnets for the End of Modernity | 11

I Confinement | 12
Fallow 1 | 12
Age of New | 13
Disposed | 14
Matters of Fact | 15
Earthy | 16

II Body, Blood & Time | 17
Bread and Stone | 17
Optimist | 18
The Heart | 19
Resistance Redefined | 20
Our Golgotha | 21
The Body | 22

III *Perichoresis* | 23
Pause | 23
Harpagmos | 24
Feathers | 25
Presuppose | 26
Germinating | 27

IV Sublime Imagination | 28
Apology | 28
Ego | 29
Your Song | 30
Timeless | 31
Rooftops | 32
Whole | 33

V My Treasures | 34
Dying | 34
Kindling | 35
Locket | 36
Transparent | 37
Treasure | 38

VI Transparency | 39
Straw Men | 39
Disciple | 40
Consummation | 41
Faces | 42
Grow | 43

VII The Doors of Perception | 44
Patience | 44
Problem | 45
Conscience | 46
Reason | 47
Harrowed | 48
Personality | 49

VIII Battles, Bread & Wine | 50
Fights | 50
The Good Fight | 51
Revolutionary | 52
Tribal Dance | 53
Sacrament Pause | 54

IX Idols are Distractions are Idols | 55
Sensation | 55
Affluenza | 56
Smart | 57
Break Your Idols | 58
The Great Conspiracy: Human Evil | 59
The Great Conspiracy: Human Goodness | 60

X Incarnation | 61
A Christmas Carol | 61
Christmas Day | 62
Progress | 63
Logos | 64

XI Reflections | 65
La Complainte de Rachel | 65
Reflection | 66
Hindsight | 67
Unfamiliar | 68
Implications | 69

XII Five Sonnets for the Inklings | 70
Tolkien | 70
Lewis | 71
Williams | 72
Barfield | 73
The Inklings | 74

XIII Five Sonnets for Wendell Berry | 75
Earth | 75
Water | 76
Wind | 77
Fire | 78
Agricclesia | 79

XIV Deconfinement | 80
Gospearth | 80
Catching Myself | 81
Find | 82
In Your Most Holy Chapel | 84
Mine | 85
Fallow 2 | 86

Coda: Home as People | 87
You Are My Music | 88
Honeymoon | 90
Anticipate | 91
Anniversary | 92
To My Son at Three Days | 93
Mid-Move | 94
Your Stare | 95
To My Son at Five Months | 96

Appendix of Epigraphs | 97

Dedication and Thanks

This book is dedicated to my beautiful wife, Silje and our wonderful son Gabriel. Thank you for being such a source of joy and spring of inspiration and creativity. The majority of these poems were written during the various COVID lockdowns and I am so thankful that I was able to be confined with you both. You are my home.

Thank you for Matthew Wimer and Wipf & Stock for working with me to publish this book and answering my many questions along the way. Thank you to Graham McFarlane, whose lectures and insights during my studies at London School of Theology, started the journey that led to many of these poems. Thanks also to Malcolm Guite whose poetry and teaching have opened so many of the themes and writers explored throughout this book. Thank you to the poet Nick Horgan for reading a very early draft of this book and giving invaluable feedback and encouragement. Thanks to my father Gilmour Lilly for your precise and poetically sensitive eye in proofreading this work, correcting errors and bringing the best out of many of these poems. And thanks to my whole family for your love and community. I am really thankful for the communities of family, friends, churches, colleagues and dialogue partners from which these poems arose, and I hope they can add something to the future conversations and developing thoughts of those who read them. A special thank you to the friends and writers who have written endorsements for this book. My appreciation for your encouragement and interest are beyond words. Finally, thank you reader for picking up this book, I hope that reading these poems can be an enriching and deepening experience.

Acknowledgements

Thanks to the following publications and podcasts for previously publishing or sharing some of these poems: *Across the Margin, Agape Review, Archetype, The BEZine, Calla Press, Dreich Broad, Dreich Magazine, Ekstasis, Fly on The Wall Press Webzine, Foreshadow, Green Ink Poetry, Heart of Flesh, Lothlorien Poetry Journal, Macrina Magazine, The Owen Barfield Literary Estate Blog, Paddler Press, Radix Magazine, Fevers of the Mind,* the *A Thousand Shades of Green* podcast, and *The Dead Letter Radio* podcast.

Overture: Home as Place

Legacy

There are treasures in my legacy.
Troves of endless worlds,
tightly enveloped in themselves,
waiting to be unfurled,
to flutter an invitation
into a dynamism beyond
any mere object.

Bound in leather and ordered,
patiently silent,
content to hold their breath
and all their secrets of layered wonder
until a searcher unfolds them,
and enters.

They have written their interweaving stories
onto my double helix
and given my feet flight.
They have signed their name into
the wet concrete of my foundations.
They call from centuries past and
from this very moment.
They are always being written,
as am I.

At Sea

"Look here, you who say, "Today or tomorrow we are going to a certain town and will stay there a year. We will do business there and make a profit." How do you know what your life will be like tomorrow? Your life is like the morning fog—it's here a little while, then it's gone."

James 4:13–15

We are all at sea.
The horizon is fluid,
its mountains are
ever changing.
Squalls bring tomorrow
into now.
We intertwine our limbs
into the rigging
and hope the waves
don't tear us at the seams,
as the celestial force of time
crashes over our bows
and threatens our creaky hull
with a premature eternity.

We are all at sea.
Planning our routes by
liquid landmarks.
Adrift in a stillness
that stretches today
into starvation.
We sink our teeth

into the decks
and hope for waves
to vibrate in our gums.
Our souls thirst for wind,
to catch our sails and move us,
from an eternal moment
into change.

A-Perfect

Only in paintings do birds fly in perfect-V.
When I look up there's always a dent in their structure.
A-symmetrical.

I remember junior school.
These imperfections must be caused
by a swapping of the avant-guard,
a sharing of slipstreams.
A-perfection.

Though it might just be
because these birds are real.

I wonder how a painting might capture my face,
soothe all the misshapen misgivings,
this damned flaking skin.
Imperfect.

I think of how, younger, I painted what is now my present,
in plans and day dreams.
Those straight lines converging in an eventual and inevitable
Arrival.

But, in breathing, the parousia of every convergence is shattered by
an enduring, a domesticity, a tangibility,

A perfection.

Spring

Winter has hidden its frosty face
for another few months of future.
We stand with heels in the snow,
and toes touching the thaw.
Wet, green, and flowing.
Fresh as a spring on timid skin.
Wanting the crystalline cling of water
to give into its moving.
For the brittle to become a torrent,
and to be carried in current
to another here, where
the spring light can change everything.

Autumn Home

I've found autumn again
in this country where winter
is just a space between scorches.
My short commute is now rural.
The foliage is red, orange, and falling.
Collecting in windswept clumps,
natural throw-rugs along the curb,
blocking the drains with wet leaves without life.
Here it's vineyards.
Surrounded by the ever-pastel-green
of Mediterranean pines.
They mutter of a more northerly climate,
the four distinct seasons of my home.
And they whisper of the tannins and earthy notes of my. . .
my home.

Home is in the colors of leaves,
not the species of plants.
Home is in the changing flavors
of what the earth brings forth.
It never colonizes.
It can root in new soil,
yet never lets go of the old.
Thus the map of home can widen,
not with empire,
but the expansion of its own definition.

Imagine the Water

Imagine the water rushing,
tugging at the loose soil cliff-face
of sheets of black slate,
and grey rocks like knots
in a sanded beam of earth.

Imagine it running where you stand,
changing the shape of the banks,
that display a frozen moment,
a photograph of scattering seed,
and the exposed roots of thirsty trees
stunted by the summer's dry.

Imagine that burnt book of leaves
caught in the dark colander of barky roots
racing in the new rush
of quickly falling rains,
rushing waters,
washing currents,
drying stream-beds.

Imagine the force
smoothing this stumbling wilderness
into the peaty garden path
that beckons you take off your shoes
to feel the earth.

Imagine the steam rising from the burning bush
as it evaporates the downpour,
and speaks of emancipation.

You Are His Place

He breathes from your lungs
as you from our atmosphere.

He hears the heavy thudding
of your heart through the liquid,

A constant music to accompany
our muffled voices.

He cries silently with
eyes crunched like soft tissues.

He has your nose,
he has a heart that claps in quickness,
he has a brain that recognizes
the touch of your interior,
he knows when you're sleeping
and when I caress you both.

He is present.
He is, at present, cocooned.
He will presently be ready
to see our eyes
and, through our gaze,
begin to understand
who he is.

Poems and Sonnets
for the End of Modernity

I Confinement

Fallow 1

"The cycle of hope and disappointment lies at the heart of consumer capitalism."

Clive Hamilton

Fallow from lockdown's imposed repose,
so long overdue for the depleted
human soil of a system self-disposed.
Ever consume or be defeated,
ever post online or be deleted,
empty promises are ever repeated.
A pause, a long breath, a deep shame exposed.

That this system is a cannibal
feeding and feeding on the human whole,
fearing that the crudeness of capital
is not compatible with the human soul.
Using dread of invisible enemies
to distract from great emergencies

and continual displacement of burnt out refugees;
more casualties of a cannibal structure
whose exposed shame is this secret let loose,
that the snake eating its own tail
is not eternal, but a tightening noose.

Age of New

My feet skip on the pavements
of our rapid innovations.

As if the printing press was invented every month
one letter at a time.

Ripples of introspection expand in concentric circles
as each discarded model disappears beneath the surface.

We are the liquid,
that mysterious ambience
with the dark sheen of night water.

And we keep inventing things
that sink.

Disposed

You marvel at the colors
as the sun sets
into the cess pool.
At the colors, and the stench.

There is life
in the decomposition.
Primitive life
thriving on death,
as only life can.

It is not a circle in balance,
but a never ending parade of ants
trafficking fragments of corruption
into the rush-hour city subway system
of their over-populated nests.

Matters of Fact

Matters of fact drive this engine
that digs our graves,
deep and permanent,
below the layered sediment
of our sewage pipes, foundations,
tarmac, paint and plastic.
They fit on the back of a postage stamp,
and replace it with digital instancy.
Patience has gone the way of the letter,
and the spirit knows it is alone.

They give you new eyes to notice
the blades in the ploughs,
the money in the dirt.
But ignore the nothing that it gives
so endlessly to us
and our land,
and the self-assured damnation
we will go into, rich and empty,
as a screen without juice.

Earthy

Important poems overdress
like rich teenagers at the mall
between lockdowns.
The poor look on in disbelief.
'How many meals are lost
on those shoes, in which are feet
uncalloused and sanded to
a pink and soft uselessness?'

Closer to the soil,
with the space to breathe
and dig for earthworms,
are the words with dirty fingernails.
Like a toddler,
amazed at each fresh syllable,
the way new dexterity
tastes on the tongue.

These sprout stanzas
and bloom into something living.

II Body, Blood & Time

Bread and Stone

What are the questions that rattle around
needling inside your empty stomach,
making friends with that hungry growling sound,
that echoes and accuses, rings and aches?
And what is the bleached loaf you're feeding it?
A beautiful stone that shatters the teeth,
dead, disenchanted, with nothing beneath.
An ornament of a placated grief
that starts by giving, as a long-con thief
and establishes a shallow belief,
so quickly extinguished, to then bequeath
a famished bewildered dust, repeating it.
You cannot live as a struggling stone.
Break bread together, yet not bread alone.

Optimist

"The correct response to uncertainty is myth making."

Dr. Martin Shaw

I don't think this system will survive
but that does not make me a pessimist.
Doomsday prophecies always sound contrived
though we stand at the edge of a precipice.
We are also crawling, desperate and damp
out of a stagnant, decomposing hell,
an everlasting plastic, synthetic swamp
of discarded marrow and treasured shells.
We blink in the light of possible new,
with our imaginations still subdued
we cannot yet find a shape to construe
an alternative to what we always knew.
But to grow one must relinquish security
and a system's death brings opportunity.

The Heart

"It is not the religious act that makes the Christian, but participation in the sufferings of God in the secular life."

Dietrich Bonhoeffer

Epochs, economies and proud empires
rise from the ashes of our last idols,
and burn unwitting in self-made fires
which forged the crown of tomorrow's rule.
In the midst of this spiraling folly
the human heart sits proud and regal
radiating a deep melancholy,
its eternal potential for good or evil.
These epochs, empires and economies
change not the doom of the placid human heart,
they merely build to destroy, with ease,
promising all, delivering not a start.
But once, change appeared in a giving loss,
creator subverting all this on the cross.

Resistance Redefined

Joy is resistance in a world of stress.
Peace is resistance in the midst of war.
When all claim perfection in shallow allure
resistance is to openly confess
our weakness and faults, to lay them all bare.
When you're called a consumer, live simply.
Where greed is praised resistance is to share.
Amidst propaganda, resistance is honesty.
Surrounded by ego-echo-chambers
resistance is to cross the wide divide
to breathe the perspective of other cultures.
Resistance is to protect the other side.
In a world of competition and gain
resistance is to choose to bear another's pain.

Our Golgotha

". . .And there the logical hook
On which the Mystery is impaled and bent
Into an ideological Instrument."

Edwin Muir

The hills that we have chosen to die on
are the foothills of that cursed mountain,
where Molech claimed his sacrifice from
and the blood from the soil is still shouting.
The blood of the innocent questioners
chased away from their homes just for asking.
The blood of the truths, in two we sectioned,
of the halves we kept and the lies they're masking.
And the blood of the halves we discarded;
beauty, imagination and silence.
These our didactic souls disregarded
as we made a home of smiles and violence.
With this simple truth, turn your idols over:
We should die on no hill but Golgotha!

The Body

Dehumanization facilitates
cutting off our own ears to tend our hate
that shows itself in patronizing claims
more often than drawing and taking aim.
Hospitality is disarmament,
it's clearing pretense from our ear canal,
knowing that no perspective is banal,
making room for mutual nourishment,
letting all five senses bask in presence,
softening the echoing walls of our cave,
seeing the being behind how one behaves,
asking questions first of our own essence.
It's knowing Christ is incarnate inside
loving humility not defensive pride.

III *Perichoresis*[1]

Pause

Resistance is an open door within
the imagination, for tomorrows
undreamt of amidst our mundane sorrows,
and distant fallout from our affluent sin
of indifference because of distance.
The roots of living plants seep nutrients
into soils exhausted by incongruence
of perpetual harvest without a chance
of repose. When questions of production
are deemed irrelevant for a moment.
To stop. Appreciate the slow movement
of breathing beauty beyond mere function.
Night to night pours forth speech in silence sweet,
in muted awe we make the choir complete.

1.. *Perichoresis* (περιχώρησις) is a Greek term for an inter-participatory dance, that has been used to express the relationship between the Three Persons of The Trinity since the early fathers.

Harpagmos[2]

Deep breath. You cannot change anyone.
Let go. Let go. Let go the need to speak.
Let it roll from off the back of your tongue
to disperse along limbs you thought were weak,
to drip out from your calloused finger tips,
and the strength of youth will reignite in you.
For time threatens with a narrowing view
as mortality's shadow does eclipse
potential's celestial embers glow
in slowing walls of broken circumstance.
Eyes screwed shut we tightly grip what we know
in our grasping we seek significance.
Deep breath. Let go. Find such peculiar wealth
in living life for so much more than self.

2.. *Harpagmos* (Ἁρπαγμός) is the Greek word for the act of seizing or the thing being seized. It is the root of the word used by Paul in Philippians 2:6, which the NRSV translates as '. . .who, though he was in the form of God, did not regard equality with God as something to be *exploited*. . .'

Feathers

*"If space is made of superstrings,
Then God's a knitter, everything
Is craft. . ."*

Gwyneth Lewis

We were right. We always had to be.
We chiseled both the rock and hard places
to break it all down to its components.
Now we are stuck between two great quarries
interned in those atoms up to our faces,
choking on the dust of our achievements.
Listen, as these pebbles fuse together
drawn in by strings through many dimensions,
resounding the chord struck at creation,
singing in us the notes of elation,
rousing our sedated apprehension,
to understand our nature as feathers:
Alone; a delicate, beautiful thing.
United; a great and unfolding wing.

Presuppose

Invented labels exclude the animate,
imposed identities kill dialogue,
all broadcasting fine tuned monologue
defining the danger in the desperate.
Competition beating conversation,
this social distance becomes a living
tragic metaphor in repetition
for humanity, bereft of giving.
Draining the other from our essence
is to banish the Spirit from our breath,
pneuma without *pneuma*, a living death.[3]
To become absent, even in presence.
This denial of basic humanity
paves the way for untold atrocity.

3.. *Pneuma* (πνεῦμα) is the Greek word that can be translated as spirit, breath or wind depending on the context. Owen Barfield explored the significance of this in his book *Poetic Diction*.

Germinating

*"Let me walk beside the scents
Of new and unknown petals in bloom."*

James Berry

I was never a reluctant poet.
I grasp the pen before I would concepts,
plant a naïve seed of complete precepts
without the capacity to follow it
to its leafy conclusion, venomous,
and suited to merely one climate.
Oh how I wish I could hibernate
from responsibilities, pernicious,
to dream of seeds that would collect themselves
and share their vibrant secrets between shells.
So cold and brittle, so easy to breach,
to germinate ideas that can teach,
and rejoice in full imagination
the shoots of an open apprehension.

IV Sublime Imagination

Apology

"...and last of all he appeared to me also, as to one abnormally born."

1 Corinthians 15:8

*"We must feel
the pulse in the wound
to believe..."*

Denise Levertov

Logical positivism reaches
its end, not only in implied contradiction.
But when one, stripped of all pretense, searches
the verifiable fact from fiction,
one discovers the best explanation
of historical evidence gives way
to meaning beyond the empirical.
Reason behind the reason of the day
demands you be open to miracles,
for consciousness precedes observation,
like a map drawn from a half lucid dream
guides you through what you have not yet seen.
The closed system cracked by living leavened bread:
Encounter Jesus, risen from the dead.

Ego

"Yet a feather does not fly of its own accord, but the air bears it along. And I, like the feather, am not endowed with great powers or human education, nor do I even have good health, but I rely wholly on God's help."

Hildegard of Bingen

The ego is a phantom polluting
the spirit within all good intentions.
Forever it whispers, convoluting
selfless acts with arrogant pretension.
As believers boasting of being depraved
proud that their nature's not worth being saved,
with corrupted humility, blaming,
excluding, and self-righteously self-shaming.
This is 'i am', twisted and distorted
while the great I AM is being itself,
giving of himself celestial wealth
without asking what can be afforded.
Tasted by the touching souls of lovers;
to be, is to be something for others.

Your Song

"I'll know my song well before I start singing"

Bob Dylan

My crystal melody, in frictioned movement ringing,
its significance will burn in my bones,
a purpose, a path, for my feet alone
to walk this circled staircase, spiraling.
Without a third dimension, I'll just trace
the melody footprints of my refrain
over and over, redrawing my face,
retelling my tale, respelling my name.
As important as my purpose may be
my ears alone drain its potency,
for there is nothing real in prophecy
that can't impact another's melody.
So we'll mingle like notes in the finest wine,
I'll know your song well 'fore I start singing mine.

Timeless

"...as imagination bodies forth
The forms of things unknown, the poet's pen
Turns them to shapes..."

William Shakespeare

Gradual change is always everywhere,
yet real transformation is truly rare.
It came with the phonetic alphabet,
with the invention of Gutenberg's press,
and now, breathing within the internet,
we live in the wake of endless access.
Entrepreneurs are 'men of the hour'
innovators 'ahead of their time'
but more profound than profit or progress
is what can be truly named as timeless.
Eternal resounding in mortal rhyme,
newborn gurgling transcendent power.
Timeless transformation touches our bones
as The Word bodies forth what was unknown.

Rooftops

"The sublime may be sensed in things of beauty as well as in acts of goodness and in the search for truth. The perception of beauty may be the beginning of the experience of the sublime. The sublime . . .is the silent allusion of things to a meaning greater than themselves."

Abraham Joshua Heschel

These quiet rooftops contain everything,
now that we've internalized our markets
our entertainment and our pretending,
our hiding, our show, our scheduled targets.
Forgotten the rhythm of crashing waves,
the dry crackle of crushed autumn leaves,
from within synthetic, platonic caves;
a home, a hole, a portal to be pleased.
But, far above these rooftops, poetry
flies south under cloud, in perfect-V
and in the silence of breakdown, beauty
returns to deserted streets, noisily.
Guard your hope indoors and you'll be kept
safe through all risks of living, while you've slept.

Whole

"Prayer...
God's Breath in man, returning to his birth..."

George Herbert

Eternity always touches today
and each shadow contains a spark of death.
yet, from permanence we look the other way,
ever possessive of our borrowed breath,
without knowing how much it's really worth
we choose not to return it to its birth.
In steel trap lungs it transforms to toxic
dioxide, draining strength in narcotic
sedation, until we simply dissolve,
the rich, poor, high, low, incorporeal
emptied of spirit, mere flesh unabsolved.
Oh who this severed being can heal?
To allow my lungs to reach my soul
and, in denying Plato, make me whole.

V My Treasures

Dying

". . .Each bird was tagged like cattle with one word
And they burned them in to my mind, they read:
You have never lived because you have never died."

Dan Smith

Accept death's inevitability
and you will leave your journey's first boot-print,
for you cannot face your vulnerability
while holding your breath. Light to make you squint
won't burst through grey clouds, to abate that storm
of nothing, growing in the pit of you.
But you will know all tempests are of one form
and each time you blink you'll see through to blue.
You can stop chasing inert distractions,
extract pretense from the present and live,
taste the deathlessness in your interactions,
take the mirror from your vision and give.
If you're stuck ignoring or fighting death
the mind will be forever bound in breath.

Kindling

"The spiritual life is one of continuing to begin every day with a question."

Scott Cairns

Follow the infinite regress of these
dependent definitions, and we find
either a lostness or fullness of mind.
Neither outcome was synthesized to please.
What is death? What is life? And personhood?
What grounds the pregnant earth of gardens?
From whence springs the living soul of neighborhood?
How can human hearts so quickly harden?
Find a chaste grace here, in open questions.
A tenderness, as from a curious
infant, exploring innate suggestions,
whose bare words unveil the mysterious.
Here is the kindling of consciousness,
partaking in the flame, pure and deathless.

Locket

Those little pictures inside jewelry
never portray a violent victory,
a triumphant political party,
a boost in the national economy.
Behind such delicate silver fastenings
secret photos of faces are treasured
whose value, in gold, cannot be measured,
shared or compared, for they are a hastening
of the flavor of timelessness in time,
a frozen moment, a window framing
an ageless portrait whose perception, blind,
changes not with the wearers own waining.
Achievements are counted, put on display,
love's treasures are hidden, safe and away.

Transparent

All my little disgraces are littered
where I should now prepare my nourishment.
They are the spilt coffee grains, that wilted
morning fingers, a feeble dirigent,
let miss their mark. Now they are but black sand
whose caffeine no longer has relevance.
I must kiss the darkened benevolence
of fully dwelling here, where my feet stand,
before my well-intentioned detritus.
Seeing, accepting, owning, and cleaning.
For what am I? but a clumsy fetus
damaging the womb without meaning.
It does us no good to become our hurt
or deny the existence of our dirt.

Treasure

"...Life comes through the cross, and only the one who lives this way is truly a human being."

Fr. John Behr

Growth is as real as is repetition,
one does not disprove the other, for yet
the spiral of our pride and contrition,
though it may be forgetful, does beget
courage in the midst of hottest hellfire,
cowardice during a heavenly bliss.
Humility wrought, not in sword and fist,
emerges from our flesh as it expires
and all the learning from all this suffering,
from all this pleasure and all we measure
might coalesce in our free offering,
accepting one cannot own true treasure
while lives orbit around retaining health.
We break the circle in dying to self.

VI Transparency

Straw Men

*"All silencing of discussion is an assumption of infallibility...
few think it necessary to take precautions against their own
fallibility."*

John Stuart Mill

Straw men keep dispersing in the tempest.
Easy to build from tattered personhood,
their entrails clog our drains and they infest
our humanity with misunderstood
means from misjudged, mislabeled intentions.
We're more entrenched with each new invention,
echo chambers seizing our attention.
Our harvest is kept safe from circling crows,
our souls self-deprived of what helps them grow,
our soils dense with what we already know.
Identities dig the deepest trenches
calling it plowing, armed with pretensions.
Soundbites are clumsily fired mortar shells
and from this pride we construct our own hells.

Disciple

"And Jesus saith unto him, The foxes have holes, and the birds of the air have nests; but the Son of man hath not where to lay his head."

Matthew 8:20

The disciple's identity is not
simply progressive or conservative.
Conserve what is just and noble and true,
progress into greater justice and truth.
Burn past arrogance, the empire and rot,
resist the march to the prerogatives
of the day, obsessed with what is new.
Beware the small print of your loyalties
that try to justify atrocities,
sacrificing for the greater good,
dehumanizing one who disagrees
and transforming fervor into wormwood.
Foxes have their holes and birds have their nests,
but the Son of Man had nowhere to rest.

Consummation

"Could I ever get enough of you?
. . .
Vivid more vivid, real more real.
I stare towards heavens you reveal."

Micheal O'Siadhail

Delicacies are shared in this silence
that mean so much more than vocalized thought.
To measure our afterglow with science
and numbers is to count one's breath as bought,
yet everything meaningful is immune
from an economy, crashed and burning.
When tired spirits ache sweetly and in tune
to a deepening of patient yearning
an overcoming of the constancy,
the droning demand for contingency
plans is drowned out by naked honesty,
and dignifying vulnerability.
The crisis of our age is overcome
when, from the pretense of masks, we are undone.

Faces

We live behind perfect profile pictures,
pixels portraying polished, plain portraits.
Our acned mind might think them just fictitious,
lifeless and powerless over our fates,
but they are an ugly, suckling ivy,
sucking nutrients from our vertebrae.
An animated scaffolding, subtly
dismantling the breath, so gradually,
from the architecture of complexity,
the organic artwork of our faces,
the dark beauty of personality,
the wisdom of our innermost places.
In taking the risk of fading to black
our skulls can start to grow our faces back.

Grow

*"Time is a game
played beautifully
by children."*

Heraclitus

When you're sharing time with an infant
you can either choose to be productive
or you can choose to grow, be constructed.
You cannot do both. For to be in front
of such vibrant unfiltered presence
is to be confronted by your own absence.
The fickle, flammable nature of your
to-do lists, timetables, pastimes and chores.
And each irritable response bursting,
reacting to pure curiosity,
is a moment that reciprocity
can still your pride and quench your soul's thirsting.
Open your fingers, let deadlines slip through.
Grow! The child you're raising is teaching you.

VII The Doors of Perception

Patience

Corruption of our primitive prowess
haunts every domain of progression.
The fossils of obsolete virtuosity
and cadavers of cultures are countless,
hidden in sedimented succession,
endless layers of unyielding history.
We marvel at the ancient fingers
wielding stone as the mouse does the cursor,
and at the families of yesteryear
whose un-captured eyes could yet still linger,
be reciprocated by another's
and, in hand written patience, draw near.
Convenience is a poisonous womb
birthing new wonders that keep us entombed.

Problem

Embodying contradictions, we sit
a wet sack of tensions, pushed to bursting.
A complex miracle of deficit
wherein every moment could be nursing
a new germinating simplicity,
a tenure-free flourishing,
a monolithic multiplicity
broadcasting the hope of diminishing,
and a converging disinclination
to meet, like the wet noses of stray dogs
sharing whatever fleas, whatever drugs,
fur-thickened skin deflecting defamation.
Solve now the hard problem of consciousness,
be eaten by your own hypothesis.

Conscience

Not all of our contradictions are
laudable tensions to be sat in and
stirred by. Fear can pull your gaze from afar
and crown a tyrant with a magic wand,
a silver tongue, an opportunist wit,
a bag of good reasons and a desire.
Weighed down by trinkets, we sink in the pit,
freeze in the glacier, burn in the fire.
Our own capacities tie us in knots,
yet growing within is the miracle,
the little answer to our broken lot.
Buried below, we find the pinnacle.
The apex of the earth is inside us
with the power to unite or divide us.

Reason

*". . .Poetry is that
which arrives at the intellect
by way of the heart."*

R. S. Thomas

Our age has produced useless metaphors,
innumerable and all misdirections.
Invented dichotomies lead towards
an overdue mental insurrection,
for the universe has become so small,
turning as it does on a broken tooth,
that Paleolithic knife edge. The fall:
A storm, trapped in a glass jar. And truth?
Pinned to the polystyrene by reason,
unmoving, examinable and grey.
Always grey, in an endless damp season
where emotion has been shackled away.
Logic that considers all but feelings
considers us not as human beings.

Harrowed

Speak me into existence, I am yours.
Or, the you that is yet to be. Transformed by
the speaking, the creative change that pours
from the wellspring of language. As the tide,
unstoppable and incessantly true.
Yet warm, as the most familiar embrace.
there is a great light in the future's view,
and new terrain for the radiance of grace
to display across fresh contours, shadows
exquisite, and abstractly portraying
the inner-workings of the artist's soul
in ecstatic breath, a visual praying.
For all our doom, we yet have tomorrow,
a landscape of soil, freshly harrowed.

Personality

"I know of no other Christianity and no other Gospel than the liberty both of body & mind to exercise the Divine Arts of Imagination."

William Blake

The feelings you're chasing are stained
on surfaces. Just the ink of the words.
The thin residue of the artist's pained
personality marking the absurd
on the canvas. The scab on the skin.
The news room smile. The melodic refrain.
A doorway. An embrace. A beginning.
We each have a violent vengeance within,
many and righteous, from which we abstain,
and dark, brooding compassion, restraining
our vindictive entrails with humane skin.
We are a mess of history, engrained.
All this is not exhaustive of our parts,
And our whole? A yet greater work of art.

VIII Battles, Bread & Wine

Fights

"Men will clutch at illusions when they have nothing else to hold onto."

Czesław Miłosz

Presuppositions, carrots, sticks and stones.
Break my bones. Re-mortgage my fractured home.
A system built on never ending loans
will divide against itself and implode.
It's hard to kick against the fiscal goads,
but people remain people, even so.
There comes a time when they will seek themselves
and find their shelves of purchases to be
their allocated eternal dwelling,
as decided by the salesmen who delve
into new definitions of this free
Doom. Despite the great reckoning welling
in the hearts of the masses, wound up tight,
the violence sparked will not be the good fight.

The Good Fight

*"I'll fight your rope, your rules, your hope
As your sparrow does under your super-
vision!"*

Jack Mapanje

The good fight is not in the violence
but the grueling daily grind of being
fully present. Movable in silence
and in shouting. Invisibly seeing
the power behind the play, and playing.
But taking the game from the arena
and into the sand-pit where it belongs.
Noticing the blood, tending the lesions,
both broken nose and cut knuckle. Weighing
not the trifling arrest and subpoena
but the breath, every note of tragic songs,
and every synthesized social adhesion.
Bandwagons of revolution comply.
if your hope is in them, it's already died.

Revolutionary

"There is one thing, and only one thing, in which it is granted to you to be free in life, all else is beyond your power: that is to recognize and profess the truth."

Leo Tolstoy

To be a revolutionary is to
let your living make the mightiest noise,
not to write a message of peace in blood,
or let a movement's leader dictate to you.
It's not to find the tribe that fits your voice
but to reject tribalism for good,
as a concept and as a condition.
You don't prove your not a pig by grunting
in protest against the proposition.
You must be changed to be change to see change,
and know the bed-rock of what you're wanting
beneath the gargantuan mountain range
of rough rubble reasons rabble rousing,
To the meat of the hope you're espousing.

Tribal Dance

Gather around the fire, beat the drum,
tell ancient stories in the flickering.
Sing to the embers as the strings are strummed,
before this heat, exhale your bickering.
In efficacious coming together
dance! Raise the dust! Defy the weather!
But, let it be the rhythm of the cosmos
and the narrative of the fertile sparks,
the melodies in which all tongues can share,
the peace defying selfishness in loss
and mutual courage, as each embarks
to dance in the footsteps of boundless care.
Then calm this feasting in quiet divine,
transcend your elements with bread and wine.

Sacrament Pause

"taste
bread at Emmaus
that warm hands
broke and blessed."

Denise Levertov

Something hidden in daily elements.
A splint for our dualistic epoch,
Catching the fracture, treating the ailments
Rallying all spirit, stopping the clock.
Allowing time to beat within the chest
Meters that defy the pressure to be
Everything. Rather, a rhythm of rest.
Nails that fasten bread to eternity,
Torrents that wash out sickness from inside,
Poured wine whose notes fix the wandering mind
Anchored in a misty ocean of blind,
Unseeing but sure, not drifting in tide.
Something hidden in elements mundane.
Eat this meal, let your whole self be remade.

IX Idols are Distractions are Idols

Sensation

". . . You've got to keep them pretty scared, because unless they're properly scared and frightened of all kinds of devils that are going to destroy them from outside or inside or somewhere, they may start to think, which is very dangerous. . ."

Noam Chomsky

Sensationalism is a symptom,
but so are the sensations fracturing
the brittle skeleton of an eclipsed
moment, as everyone sees through crimson
panic. Is it the manufacturing
of crisis, or the dark apocalypse?
The theater stage, or the cancer ward?
The studio, or the battle field?
The propaganda or, the living breath?
As liberty is labelled untoward
to deadly diversions the future yields,
and shall we partake in incarnate death?
Poles apart, aghast in horrored wonder,
partisan tribes tear the truth asunder.

Affluenza

"The impetus of consumption, just like the impulse of freedom, renders its own gratification impossible."

Zygmunt Bauman

We are at the mercy of the weather,
toiling, exposed to the elements.
Cultivating want, simulating need,
self-congratulating, for no good deed
is done without analyzed investment
of return for a risky endeavor.
But it all comes to pieces in the storm,
it's infected by the brand new illness
trapping us inside our luxury,
and we all come to pieces as we swarm
to shopping centers whose eery stillness
is disenchanted by mad puppetry.
A frenzy of purchase denies the drought
and it's this that'll make the water run out.

Smart

*". . .the prisoners look like
Marionettes hooked to strings of light."*

Yusef Komunyakaa

It's not just the watch, the purse, the book.
It's the talisman, the rosary,
the touching point, and the eight-ball you shook.
It's the zemi of mental security,
ever present, it's the phylactery
holding the zealot's personality.
The voodoo doll, cursing in the spirit
with mystical power, this amulet
keeps your gaze while running on battery.
And inside? The imaginarium.
Trapped in apps, worlds of boundless invention
sedated, alongside identity.
Pry it from your fingers, just you alone
can master this menace taking your home.

Break Your Idols

Break your idols, tear them asunder
Reek a soulful revenge on their wonder.
Every mirrored surface bids your lost gaze
And you must smash them to reveal their blades.
King of your own altar, burn to cinders
Your throne. How it sits neatly in your palm.
Own the imperfections you airbrush out,
Untie your mind from this comforting harm.
Rampage and write, reveal your voice and shout,
Indignant of the deep social control
Deified inventions impose on souls
Oblivious to the sickness they extol.
Living flesh, so vulnerably breathing,
Savor the air these idols are thieving.

The Great Conspiracy: Human Evil

"If only there were evil people somewhere insidiously committing evil deeds, and it were necessary only to separate them from the rest of us and destroy them. But the line dividing good and evil cuts through the heart of every human being. And who is willing to destroy a piece of his own heart?"

Alexandr Solzhenitsyn

The great conspiracy is deep within
simmering beneath the varnished veneer,
lying in wait to take the nearest reins
to control the fate of all would-be peers.
It's the opportunistic urge to grasp
the slender throat whose goose-pimpled skin
is exposed by circumstance, and who gasps
at the same crises strength uses to win.
This conspiracy, old as humanity
needs not a secretive infrastructure
to perpetually maim and fracture.
The truth behind the illuminati
is the darkness lurking behind all eyes,
a parasite with a human disguise.

The Great Conspiracy: Human Goodness

"For when the weakness of the flesh is absorbed, it manifests the Spirit as powerful; and again, when the Spirit absorbs the weakness, it inherits the flesh for itself, and from both of these is made a living human being."

Irenaeus of Lyon

The great conspiracy is deep inside
beneath the overt nonchalant display,
self conscious despair and subconscious pride.
An image, an imprint, an infant
participating in the will that chose
to give life, the abundance of being
surrounding, permeating, and seeing
through the opaque winter cold, keeping closed
the outside eyes from apprehending
that there is a darkness, a light, and a choice,
to peel back the layers of pretending,
to find the echo of the still small voice.
There is a goodness respiring within,
true humanity trying to begin.

X Incarnation

A Christmas Carol

We are living in A Christmas Carol.
A million Bob Cratchets man the stores
keep the tills ringing, and polish the floors,
though maybe in more modern apparel
for a groomed appearance is a basic
need, an essential, placed before the sun.
For this, family moments are wasted
as buying takes the place of fun,
and post-lockdown profits could be so huge.
We are living in that Charles Dickens tale
and us who shop during holiday sales
are incarnations of Ebeneezer Scrooge.
Ghosts of Christmas past, present, yet to come,
from this synthesized need, cure everyone.

Christmas Day[4]

"Not the intense moment
Isolated, with no before and after,
But a lifetime burning in every moment
And not the lifetime of one man only
But of old stones that cannot be deciphered."

TS Eliot

Please come, feel the cracks in my Christmas Day
and I will show you a string of moments.
Flawed, perfect, precious, peculiar.
Threaded together in fiery play
by a single golden ray. Fulfillment
perpetual, of a joyful longing fire,
that glowing wire of eternal breath
illuminating every present's birth,
resounding in ever-glow after its death
and filling mundane memories with worth.
So much so, the outer veneer ruptures,
through fissures of each instance, eruptions
of timeless embrace overcome the fray.
Come and feel the cracks in my Christmas day.

4.. This poem was written after listening to an episode of the *Image* podcast entitled '*Touching Eternity: A conversation with Scott Cairns and Malcolm Guite*'. In the episode the two poets discuss creativity, time, developing understandings of literature and language, and how all this impacts church practice and Christian life. The Eliot quote in the epigraph was alluded to during the conversation.

Progress

"We were too busy analyzing the pictures being projected on the wall to notice that the wall itself had been sold."

Naomi Klein

Every time has its arbitrary rules,
its own red tape, its administrative
nightmares, and our age is built on paper.
We construct a purgatory with queues
and non-intrusive music, conducive
to building an atmosphere of vapor.
What great leaps forward! What development!
People are taller. Buildings live longer.
We can be anywhere and nowhere.
This self-congratulating system
distracted by its own ego, ponders
not the cost of its vanity fair.
Madly buying in vogue material
we fade into the in-ethereal.

Logos[5]

"Because He is the beginning. . . wherever He is, the world begins again."

Malcolm Guite

Changes permeate even the sameness,
but some definitions are evasive.
Some words wander, even as they're spoken.
A phonetic journey, though not aimless.
Destinations are subtly abrasive
to a mind whose caravan is broken,
standing knee deep in hard and dry concrete,
who must pull the legs from off the meanings
to have a static concept to possess.
But language is living if we don't kill it,
we enter its meandering leanings
as we speak, and gain eternal access
to the λόγος of life, pure change to entice.
Heraclitus steps in the same river twice.

5.. *Logos* (λόγος) the Greek word for 'word' and a whole lot more including 'reason' 'wisdom' 'speech' and 'account', first given specific philosophical treatment in the writings of Heraclitus, and was used to introduce something mysteriously new about Jesus in the famous prologue to John's gospel. The connection between Heraclitus, John's gospel and *Logos* are explored in a sermon by the poet and priest Malcolm Guite quoted in the epigraph. See the appendix of epigraphs for the reference to the sermon.

XI Reflections

La Complainte de Rachel

"Already we are breaking down the habits of thought which have survived from before the Revolution. We have cut the links between child and parent. . ."

George Orwell

Listen to the din of Rachel's weeping!
You want to teach my son to question every
authority and assumption, but yours.
Pluck him from his crib while he is sleeping
at the tender and trusting age of three,
seeping your laicity[6] into his pores.
Your Revolution was not just neutral,
you severed the heads and freed the masses,
yet shackled them to presuppositions
of progress without meaning. Your brutal
and malignant dogma, as time passes,
becomes the bars of incarceration.
My son's mind will be caged by no rubric,
he is not a child of the republic.

6.. Laicity (from the French Laïcité) is the constitutional principle of secularism in France, where the author has been living since 2015.

Reflection

*"Backwards I compel Gloucester to yield to change
Polis is this."*

Charles Olson

"The point of [The Narcissus] myth is the fact that men at once become fascinated by any extension of themselves in any material other than themselves."

Marshal McLuhan

We made these mansions, and their arrogance.
Our ingenuity is poured into
the painstaking production of mirrors,
increasingly elaborate elegance
to entrance eyes that were meant to see through
blemishes, now self-transfixed in error.
Earthquakes in our inner landscape occur
with each new invention of reflection.
Still waters. Polished brass. Layered smooth glass.
Pin hole cameras, spirit's shot, soul's procured.
Chemical retinas, digitized so fast.
Selfies that instantly soothe imperfections.
The history of technology is
Narcissus diving into the Polis.

Hindsight

Far from ourselves, we grow strange. Curious
of the unheard future sighing beyond
an holistic reunion. We abscond
from commenting on waves of furious
faces, the causes that will carry us
like undercurrents, to the popular
abyss, the distractions that will fake us
from questions that keep us in fresh water.
Oh how the journey will misshape our joints,
we'll crack and groan with tectonic friction,
wiser for the pain's heavy labored point
but full of regret for a gentler fiction.
From the silent throne of retirement
we will but observe youth's vigor, misspent.

Unfamiliar

". . . in consequence of the film of familiarity and selfish solicitude we have eyes, yet see not, ears that hear not, and hearts that neither feel nor understand."

Samuel Taylor Coleridge

Question every earthly authority
the way molten rock challenges mountains
with heat and glow, and a slow, considered,
hypnotic resolve. Such calamity
as is caused when the foundations fountain
through the summit, like ants ordered
to war by an innate complicity,
is not the call of being and breathing.
But to live at a different temperature.
As heat, to melt rampant duplicity.
As light, illuminate daylight thieving.
As liquid, transform our cold container.
Make strange the accepted forms of control,
for each context demands parts of your soul.

Implications

"Faites autre chose que ce qui se fait normalement dans la société, que vous ne pouvez pas modifier : il vous appartient de créer sur d'autres bases une autre société."[7]

Jacques Ellul

Always a voice of imagination,
Never swallowing the way things are
As reason enough for exploitation.
Reckoning with desensitization,
Called to believe in a love above law.
Holding to account our institutions,
Requiring deep justification:
Insufficient is 'our own interest'.
Suffering is no by-product for wealth.
Towing no line, activism is no mere gesture
It's a way of belonging somewhere else:
A kingdom where the king's doom was to die,
Negating tyranny that cares not why.
Sacraments nourish us in love, to defy.

7.. Author's translation of the French epigraph: *"Do something different from that which is usually done in society, which you cannot change anyway. It is up to you to create another society, on other foundations."*

XII Five Sonnets for the Inklings

Tolkien

"The notion that motor-cars are more 'alive' than, say, centaurs or dragons is curious; that they are more 'real' than, say, horses is pathetically absurd."

J.R.R. Tolkien

It's coming down around me as I write,
fingers tapping, shouting in near silence
documenting the divorce of sight and light.
Soundbites repeating that plagal cadence,
the 'AMEN' of a time of lines stutters,
unable to admit its finitude,
but order in the midst of chaos mutters
of monsters, withering the wealth accrued.
We are but shrapnel, outraged by the blast
that animates us. Our statements are flames
frozen from context in digital frames
from which will emerge the new ruling class.
Make your difference tiny, tangible and
slow enough to compose roots in the land.

Lewis

"To live in a fully predictable world is not to be a man."

C.S Lewis

We are remade in every moment.
Though the beaten track lies before our feet,
predestination is a temptation
rather than a given. We have movement
enough in our destinies to defeat
the map, discover a destination
inaccessible to all who would shun
the road of impossible resistance.
We have capacities to break and mend
beyond the fences of mental protection,
the zeitgeist's perpetual insistence
to delimit all one might apprehend.
Here it is, the substance that makes you more.
You're made of it! A tangible true lore.

Williams

"To love God and to love one's neighbor are but two movements of the same principle, and so are nature and grace. . ."

Charles Williams

Words must cohere to partake in *Logos*.
They have to do more than just resonate
rally, rouse, remit, reinforce and rage.
Reactions can resist co-inherence,
yet bare breath has nothing to propagate.
Inter-dependance struggles not for wage,
but is! *Pneuma*, *Logos*, *Patros*, embrace
In *Theos*.[8] A meal. A community,
a coming together to neither earn
nor spend. The source, the end, the smiling face.
The inclination to escape cities
and share a fire with other hearts that burn.
The rush that pushes you to mere function
seizes being and leaves only compunction.

8.. The four Greek words have been often used for the different persons of the Godhead: *Pneuma* (πνεῦμα) - Spirit; *Logos* (λόγος) - word; *Patros* (πατρὸς) - Father; *Theos* (θεός) - God.

Barfield

"...the poetic... that bodiless ocean of life out of which all works of art spring."

Owen Barfield

We participate in one and the same
consciousness, feeling its sudden changes.
Hark! Our keel scraping against pebbles,
the impending bed pronounces your name
in metallic whispers. Thriving dangers
well in the stomach of open rebels,
finding each other in shallow shipwrecks,
the debris of something real, run aground.
The breathing remnant of togetherness
is pregnant with salvaged sails and decks.
floating in future out of the bounds
set by an isolated consciousness.
Far from shores of nought but disagreeing,
come, let us participate in being.

The Inklings

With each new language grows an alternate
consciousness. A reversal of Babel's
curse, to transverse the impenetrable
and gain new pictures. Do not suffocate
in the closed room of one epoch's fables.
These heavy problems are soluble
in the same deep there has forever been.
Without urgency, save for slowing down,
save for partaking in the stranger's pain,
save for soaking through, from pretense, making clean
and translucent, as a wet white gown
clings to the skin. What we would hide, made plain.
When The Lord breathed language into our lungs
He gave the entwining of disparate tongues.

XIII Five Sonnets for Wendell Berry

"The energy that comes from living things is produced by combining the four elements of medieval science: earth, air, fire, and water... The technology appropriate to the use of this energy, therefore, preserves its cycles. It is a technology that never escapes into its own logic but remains bound in analogy to the natural law."

Wendell Berry

Earth

Forsaken consequence won't stay quiet.
We know that the soil cries by protest,
spitting out the seed from her new scars,
hating the soul of every new farmer,
their boots feeling just like those that harmed her.
A living tapestry to disarmament
the earth loved our slaughtered varmint.
Her dreams of shelter now made manifest,
not in grass but in the nightmare of our cars
and their tarmac. Yet she needs no armor
apart from the growing garments of green,
and any who want to farm her must mean
it, earn her trust in patience foreseen.
Knowing her as living, not mere machine.

Water

Find a body of water and submerge.
Right up to your hair. Right into your spine.
Right through to coax your spirit to emerge,
as secret minerals within this brine.
Let its integrated oneness call you
back together from your fraught dispersion,
the disenfranchisement that we crawl through,
these walls and ways, and all this inversion
of the liquid attributes of our soil
to assist the rotation of our wheels,
the opaque distance in which we embroil
our ambition for both what hurts and heals.
Find your body of water and get wet,
become all that the ripples can beget.

Wind

You were once harnessed by woven fabric,
propelling us over the rolling waves
of this blue, green, yellow, brown globe-garden,
we since have painted stark grey, with a thick
progress. Squandering the hours we'd saved
with faster transport. As the ground hardens,
we invent new fires for ancient fuels,
and textiles to protect us from your bite.
We try in vain to catch your weary sighs,
in a modern magic, we alchemize
them into energy so that we might
replace that by which our haste replaced you.
Let me be caught on the wind like litter
to dance above these inventions, bitter.

Fire

Holding the gaze and inspiring the stories
that held our culture like a fledgling,
nursing the bruised bone in that folded wing.
In the broken flickering, such glories
of a radiance at the edge of burning
cleanse the skin and simmer in the living.
Now the chick has splayed into the iron
eagle of The Reich, arrogant and dead.
We used the ashes of that ancient fire
as the foundations our towers are built on,
living by electric current instead.
Throwing fire, in conquest and desire.
Strike a match and let it catch, fan and grow.
Let dancing light illumine what you know.

Agricclesia[9]

"There are no unsacred places;
There are only sacred places
And desecrated places."

Wendell Berry

Living metaphors. Roots intertwining.
Muddy examples of incarnation.
As we make ourselves pristine with distance
we keep ourselves safe from living dependance,
growing in love with our own inventions
of metal, burning, and night time shining,
lamps that keep us from the movement of flame.
We busy ourselves with facility
to change the meaning of work and of soil,
to change the feeling of earth and our toil
to a passing of time and capital
and the use of numbers to spell our names.
Take the time to watch germinating seeds,
learn the patience to be set free indeed.

9.. The title of this poem is made by combining the word 'agriculture' and *ecclessia* (ἐκκλησία) the word usually translated as church in the New Testament. The poem was written after reflecting on Wendell Berry's Schumacher Lecture of October 24 1981, entitled 'People Land and Community' where Wendell Berry used the priorities of a healthy and functional marriage built on love to demonstrate what a healthy and functional agriculture built on love might look like, when compared to industrialized farming. As the Bible continually uses images of agriculture and marriage for the church, this led me to reflect on what the impacts of Wendell Berry's wisdom might be when applied to ecclesiology.

XIV Deconfinement

Gospearth

How beautiful is the dark earth beneath
the feet of the one who brings good news.
And how good the news of that living earth,
which rejoices in the touch of the sole.
Tributaries of irrigation bequeath
a laughing green, and budding blues
between sky, skin and soil; a new birth
in each step. Sun enticed music unfurls
from the green stem of being out of doors,
from the invisible breath within and
without us, sewing our lungs to the land,
from the vast blue of eyes turned upwards.
How beautiful is the dark earth below,
carrying good news from each seed that grows.

Catching Myself

I can't write when the bus isn't moving,
but I shuffle on ahead in my head,
hands in pockets and soles scraping the dust.
Slowly entering a future, losing
a stagnant presence with progress unsaid,
as my feet raise clouds of the planet's crust.
And I shall make a home in these moments
of re-enchantment filling my fingers
as potential words fill the ink in the pen.
I'll catch myself in a co-inherence
as the traffic eases all that lingers
in the air between the where and the when.
So, movement gets caught in moments that freeze,
like glimpsing the sunset between the trees.

Find

One day I will find, my love,
the walls that throw my voice
back at me in angry echoes,
and I'll understand.

One day I will find, my love,
the shards of words you coughed
from behind frosted glass,
convinced of your naked solitude,
and I will know you.

One day I will find, my love,
the foresight that grasps
the profound linguistics of sorrow
before it incapacitates all movement,
and I'll smile as I write.

One day I will find, my love,
the courage to clear my throat
from smalltalk and conditioning,
to whisper when all else shouts
white noise from lofty tenements,
and somehow I'll be heard.

One day I will find, my love,
the illusive realization that
my gravitational pull creates no orbit,
that the snakes circling me are after my blood,
and I'll let go of my significance.

One day I will find, my love,
memory enough to hold
the message from repeated lessons
that no longer need repeating,
and I'll grow and inch in height.

One day I will find, my love,
every golden calf in this dilapidated mansion
weathered by their own decorations,
I'll soak the place with petrol,
burn away the chaff of trinket shackles,
and I'll be able to move.

One day I will find, my love,
the secret password
to the mind of every tortured soul,
and I'll never be lost for words.

One day I will find, my love,
the hopeless wanderers' potential
buried beneath every conscious effort to forget
by following footprints that could stain a dirt road,
and I'll care not for paths.

One day I will find, my love,
the answer to all desired emancipation,
transform perspective from
my empty hands to theirs,
and I'll escape.

One day I will find, my love,
the ability to dodge my own words,
catch the bullets of someone more significant,
and I'll die with that perspective
burying deeper than skin and sinew.

In Your Most Holy Chapel

The stained windows green
the sun's glow with
a translucent life,
the opaque veins of leaves
score, in lead outlines,
the third day of Eden.

The pillars are knotted
with the wisdom of pushing
through the earth, and
withstanding the elements.
They are growing, still, and
the fingers of their foundations
are intertwining in your dark clay.

The altar is an ancient stump
of the first hewn pillar
felled for to fashion a rood of old,
felted with a soft moss and,
from the unnumbered rings that count
back to the first turning season,
shoots of living emerald protrude
seeming naked as the folded young
leaves are still damp with
the life of their grafted stem.

The table is already set,
the sacrifice is all ready...

Mine

Shining in silt,
marvels glisten through the water.
Gems like eyes like gems.
Competition would mount them
in golden clasps.
But they are natural,
and belong, embedded
in the beautiful mud.

Fallow 2

". . .And when she will take back from us all her stolen sabbath's rest
We will say, on that holy day: "amen, and yes"."

David Benjamin Blower

Fallow soil is turning slowly into stone,
untilled and weather weary. Full of seeds,
full of fossils and resting unclaimed bones,
for only the dead find the sleep they need.
Jubilee is not inactivity
but its the earthy personality
of Jesus transposed into the seasons

through debts forgotten. In our broken hour
of loans and consumption, it is nothing short
of a potential incanting power
beating between all of our breath and thought.
Isolated and racing against time,
thirsty prey pants for refreshing divine
where creating, care and life intertwine.

Momentary medicine is part of the
sickness of now, that keeps us sedated.
Sink your toes in dark soil and recall
the permanence for which you were created.

Coda: Home as People

You Are My Music

For Silje

"I think of your hands. . .
Pushing off the ledge of the easy quiet dancing between us."

                                          Tracy K. Smith

We almost suffocate, pushing through that film
separating our youth from our aged rest,
where gravity cannot hinder the joy
of a thunderous heart's elation.
Our souls, against all hope, wish to remain
yet our bodies feel the irreversible
pull of time in cumbersome wearing pain.

And it is in that membrane we live our life.
Neither here nor there,
yearning for the future, yearning for the past,
breathing in the now.
Yet it is when our bodies meet our souls,
we unite in these eternal seconds,
moments you can bite into,
where the past, future and now,
recede like tired dancers
from a stage still lit with our music.
The instruments and musicians, all gone.
The stage, the crowd, the ceiling disappearing.
The music, still growing, shaping breathing
while the very earth, along with all but

sound and *pneuma*[10] is become transparent.

There we do nothing, we are melody,
harmonizing mystery made apparent
in a simple Irish term of endearment.
Mo cheol thú.[11]
You are my music.
I love you.

10.. *Pneuma* (πνεῦμα) is the Greek word that can be translated as spirit, breath or wind depending on the context.

11.. This poem was written after listening to the *Poetry Unbound* podcast by *On Being* where host and poet Pádraig Ó Tuama reflected on the Poem 'Song' by Tracy K. Smith. His reflection led him to speak of the Irish term of endearment *Mo cheol thú*, which he translated as 'You are my music'.

Honeymoon

It pulls the imagination under,
all this living.

Beneath the surface
of the possible future,

to swim and chase
darting stars

through the submerged landscape
of doubt and anticipation.

There's an open ended story
at your shoreline,

and it's getting off to
a slow and beautiful beginning.

Anticipate

She smiles at her ripening lemons
and thinks of seed and citrus smells,
of a swelling rind
and the flavor
of long awaited
breath.

She touches her stomach
and wonders of the secrets
being written in
the synapses of
her ovaries.

Finally, the lunar routine
might present its masterpiece:
a collaboration,
an entity,
an holy mystery.

Anniversary

You are always more complete
a more complete mystery
and you make a mystic out of me.
Each new day
you make an enchanted treasure map
of my expected way,
and with every moment
you bring a vibrance of feeling
to all that once was grey.
Each night I bid sleep well my love
and each morning when we greet
our sunrise in the still dark room
you are always more complete.
A more complete mystery
and you make a mystic out of me.

To My Son at Three Days

Everyone who visits
says how tiny you are,
how little and delicate.
But I do not see it.
To me, you are larger than the world.
You fill my future
with future of your own
that extends beyond my years.
You fill my vision
as I put my forehead to yours,
so close your features blur.
So close you might be able to make out mine
with your fresh eyes
adjusting to the light and the cold.
My heart is forever in my throat.
You fill it with electricity and fear,
that your potential might be stifled
by me not reaching mine.
You fill my very person with possibility.
You fill my ears with gurgles, screams and
little bated breaths.

You are enormous.
an entire universe
laying between my chin
and my navel.

Mid-Move

I haven't seen my boy since Monday,
and I know he's all grown up.
He's learned a thousand things without my help,
and I've aged ten years
weathered by the plaster blizzard
from our dissolving walls,
and all the holes I made
for us to hang our home.
Jealous of snails.
With aching feet, and plans
that move inside my cranial shell
like a colony of startled bats.

Your Stare

You have this way of staring.
A wonder,
an infancy being filled.
Some people might call it vacant,
but it is the very opposite of vacancy.
It is the silent, open-mouthed gaze
of intense and unashamed presence.
A reaction to the wonder of being,
without the pretense of show,
or the embarrassment of wanting to look
like you already know.

To My Son at Five Months

Sweat glitters your forehead
from the effort of eating.
I can see your heartbeat
pulsating the membrane beneath
your translucent hair,
white like your viking mother's.
The plates of your skull are still
fusing together,
still displaying that
diamond of vulnerability:
An open mind.

The sun shines through your pink ears
like jellyfish in turquoise water.
Your lower lip glistens from
vibrating the sound you have just learned.
Your heart-mouth is open
in an innocent curiosity
that is too young for etiquette.
You push your cheek into my nose
as if to embrace some beautiful
and incontrovertible realization,
as if to embrace the pillow for rest.

Appendix of Epigraphs

Title:

Seamus Heaney, *Station Island,* Faber and Faber, London, 1984. From the poem *Station Island XI.*

At Sea:

James 4:13–15, quoted from the New Living Translation, published by the Tyndale House Foundation.

Fallow 1:

Clive Hamilton, Richard Denniss, *Affluenza: When Too Much Is Never Enough,* Crows Nest: Allen & Unwin, 2005.

Optimist:

Martin Shaw, from the Emergence Magazine's Podcast episode 'Navigating the Mysteries' from May 24th 2022. A transcript of the podcast can be found here: *https://emergencemagazine.org/essay/navigating-the-mysteries/*

The Heart

Dietrich Bonhoeffer, *Letters and Papers from Prison: An Abridged Edition*, SCM Canterbury, Croydon, 2001.

Our Golgotha:

Edwin Muir, *Selected Poems,* Faber and Faber, London, 2008. From the poem *The Incarnate One.*

Feathers:

Gwyneth Lewis, *Sparrow Tree,* Bloodaxe, Northumberland, 2011. From the poem *The Symbolism of Ancient Sweaters.*

Appendix of Epigraphs

Germinating:
James Berry, *Windrush Songs,* Bloodaxe, Northumberland, 2007. From the poem *Running on Empty*.

Apology:
1 Corinthians 15:8, quoted from the New International Version, published by the Biblica.

Denise Levertov, *The Stream & the Sapphire,* New Directions, New York, 1997. From the poem *On Belief in the Physical Resurrection of Jesus*.

Ego:
Hildegard of Bingen, *Hildegard to Odo of Paris,* in 'The Letters of Hildegard of Bingen Volume 1' Translated by Joseph L. Baird, Oxford University Press, New York, 1994.

Presuppose:
Owen Barfield, *Poetic Diction: A Study of Meaning*, Wesleyan University Press, Middletown, 1976.

Your Song
Bob Dylan, lyrics from the song *A Hard Rain's a-Gonna Fall*, first released on the album *The Freewheelin' Bob Dylan*, Columbia Records, 1963.

Timeless:
William Shakespeare, *A Midsummer Night's Dream,* Act V, Scene I.

Rooftops
Abraham Joshua Heschel, *God in Search of Man*, Farrar, Straus and Giroux, New York, 1976.

Whole:
George Herbert, *The Complete English Poems,* Penguin, London, 2004. From the poem *Prayer*.

Appendix of Epigraphs

Dying:

Dan Smith of Listener, from the song *You have Never Lived because you have Never Died*, From the album *Wooden heart*, Tangled Talk Records, 2010.

Kindling

Scott Cairns, from episode 125 of the *At Sea with Justin McRoberts* Podcast, released on January 12, 2023.

Disciple:

Matthew 8:20, quoted from the King James Version.

Consummation:

Micheal O'Siadhail, *Love Life*, Bloodaxe, Northumberland, 2005. From the poem *For Real*.

Treasure:

Fr. John Behr, *The Role of Death in Life: A Multidisciplinary Examination of the Relationship between Life and Death*, Ed. John Behr and Conor Cunningham, Cascade, Eugene Oregon, 2015.

Straw Men:

John Stuart Mill, *On Liberty*, 1858, Enhanced Media, Los Angeles, 2016.

Grow:

Heraclitus, as translated by Brooks Haxton, *Fragments: The Collected wisdom of Heraclitus*, Penguin, London, 2001.

Reason:

R. S. Thomas, *Collected Later Poems 1988–2000*, Bloodaxe, Northumberland, 2004. From the poem *Dont' ask me. . . .*

Personality:

William Blake, *The Complete Poems*, Penguin, London, 2004. From the poem *Jerusalem*.

Fights:

Czeslaw Milosz as translated by Jane Zielonko, *The Captive Mind*, Penguin, London, 1980.

Appendix of Epigraphs

The Good Fight:

Jack Mapanje, *The Last of the Sweet Bananas,* Bloodaxe, Northumberland, 2004. From the poem *Skipping Without Ropes.*

Revolutionary:

Leo Tolstoy as translated by Constance Garnett, *The Kingdom of God is Within You*, The Cassell, New York, 1894.

Sacrament Pause:

Denise Levertov, *The Stream & the Sapphire,* New Directions, New York, 1997. From the poem *On Belief in the Physical Resurrection of Jesus.*

Sensation:

Noam Chomsky, *Media Control,* Seven Stories, New York, 1991.

Affluenza:

Bauman, Zygmunt, *Postmodernity And Its Discontents,* Polity, Cambridge, 1998.

Smart:

Yusef Komunyakaa, *Neon Vernacular,* Wesleyan University Press, Middletown, 1993. From the poem *Prisoners.*

The great Conspiracy: Human Evil:

Alexandr Solzhenitsyn, *The Gulag Archipelago: Abridged Edition,* Harvil, London, 2003.

The Great Conspiracy: Human Goodness:

Irenaeus of Lyon, Against Heresies 5.9.2.

Christmas Day:

TS Eliot, *Four Quartets,* Faber & Faber, London, 1944. From the poem *East Coker.*

For the podcast conversation between Scott Cairns and Malcolm Guite: https://imagejournal.org/2019/08/19/touching-eternity-a-conversation-with-scott-cairns-and-malcolm-guite/

Progress:

Naomi Klein, *No Logo,* Harper Perennial, London, 2005.

Appendix of Epigraphs

Λόγος:

For the Malcolm Guite sermon on the prologue to John's Gospel: *https://archive.org/details/podcast_malcolms-podcast_the-word-world-talk_1000414626676*.

La Complainte de Rachel:

George Orwell, *1984,* Penguin, London, 2008.

Reflection:

Charles Olson, *Selected Poems,* University of California Press, London, 1993. From the poem *Maximus to Gloucester, Letter 27 (withheld).*

Marshal McLuhan, *Understanding Media*, Routledge Classics, London, 2001.

Unfamiliar:

Samuel Taylor Coleridge, *Biographia Literaria, The Complete Works In Seven Volumes, Vol III,* Harper & Brothers, New York, 1854.

Implications:

Jacques Ellul, *Anarchie et christianisme,* La Table Ronde, Paris, 1998.

Tolkien:

J.R.R. Tolkien, *Tree and Leaf,* Harper-Collins, London, 2001. From the essay *On Fairy-Stories.*

Lewis:

C.S. Lewis, *Prayer: Letters to Malcolm,* Collins, Glasgow, 1977.

Williams:

Charles Williams, *The Image of the City (and Other Essays),* Apocryphile, Berkeley, 2007. From the Essay *The Way of Exchange.*

Barfield:

Owen Barfield, *Poetic Diction: A Study of Meaning,* Wesleyan University Press, Middletown, 1976.

APPENDIX OF EPIGRAPHS

Sonnets for Wendell Berry:

Wendell Berry, *The Unsettling of America,* Counterpoint Press, Berkeley, 2015.

Agricclesia:

Wendell Berry, How to be a poet. (*https://www.poetryfoundation.org/poetrymagazine/poems/41087/how-to-be-a-poet*)

For Wendell Berry's Schumacher Lecture of October 24 1981, *People Land and Community:* https://the-schumacher-lectures.simplecast.com/episodes/people-land-and-community-wendell-berry-k5MvarIk

Fallow 2:

David Benjamin Blower lyrics from the song *The Wall,* from his independently released album *We Really Existed and We Really Did This,* 2019.

You Are My Music:

Tracy K. Smith, *Life On Mars,* Gray Wolf, Minneapolis, 2011. From the poem *Song.*

For Pádraig Ó Tuama reading and reflecting on the poem: *https://onbeing.org/programs/a-poem-for-the-space-between-us/*

Milton Keynes UK
Ingram Content Group UK Ltd.
UKHW020307151024
449648UK00012B/265